ANKHOLOGY

STREET

LINGUISTICS

The

Conscious

League

Academy

Manas   Publishing

Text &Illustration by L P

Lameek _ p @yahoo .com

AHY is the god of

music.

Linguistics = put on

some AHY. I will like to

hear some AHY.

<u>AMMUT</u> is the goddess

of punishment.

Linguistics= they are

going to be AMMUT

when they get home

for breaking curfew.

What is the AMMUT

for fighting in school?

ANKHET is the goddess

protector of fresh

water.

Linguistics= I will like to have a glass of ANKHET. Buy me a bottle of ANKHET.

BANEBDJEDET is the

god of being spiritual

lord.

Linguistics = I am very

BANEBDJEDET. To be

BANEBDJEDT one must

fast and meditate.

<u>GEB</u> is the god of

earth.

Linguistics = I was born

on GEB. GEB is the

third planet from the

sun.

HATMEHIT is the

goddess of fish.

Linguistics = I do eat

HATMEHIT. Lets have

HATMEHIT for dinner.

HORUS is the god of

pharaoh.

Linguistics = Mike Tyson what HORUS of the boxing ring. Alber Einstein was HORUS of his time.

IMHOTEP is the god of

intelligence.

Linguistics = IMHOTEP

will take a person far in

life. Now a day a

person needs

intelligence

<u>ISIS</u> is the goddess of

mother hood.

Linguistics = She is

about to become ISIS.

How is the young ISIS

doing.

KHNUM is the god of

creation.

Linguistics = what are

you KHNUM. I KHNUM

the poem.

KHONS is the moon

god.

Linguistics = the KHONS is out tonight.

There a full KHONS out tonight.

<u>OSIRIS</u> is the god of

the dead.

Linguistics = the cat got hit by a car and met OSIRIS. War bring OSIRIS.

MAAT is the goddess

of justice.

Linguistics = I shall have my MAAT in court. I am going to serve MAAT to them for there wrong doing. <u>MERET</u> is the goddess

of singing.

Linguistics = Can you MERET? I like that band MERET.

MENTU is the god of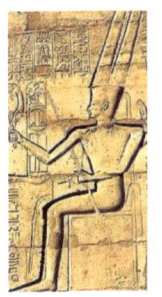

war.

Linguistics = Middle Eastern countries are

at MENTU. There
peace and MENTU
every where.

NUT Is the goddess of

the sky.

Linguistics = NUT is
very blue today. There

is a lot of stars in NUT tonight.

<u>RA</u> is the god of the

sun.

Linguistics = RA is shining today. RA is starting to set now.

SELKET is the goddess

of medicine.

Linguistics = The doctor prescribed a SELKET to me. I have to take SELKET two times a day.

SESHAT the the

goddess of science.

Linguistics = I took

SESHAT in high school.

I had to take SESHAT in

college.

<u>SET</u> is the god of storm.

Linguistics = a SET is coming tonight. Next week SET will last for three days.

SHU is the god of air.

Linguistics = Country

SHU is fresh. Mountain

SHU is thin.

<u>TAURET</u> is the goddess

of child birth.

Linguistics = She is

about to TAURET any

day now. She gave

TAURET last week to a

baby boy.

<u>TEFNUT</u> is the goddess

of rain.

Linguistics = It is

TEFNUT out side. Did it

stop TEFNUT yet?

<u>DJEHUTY</u> Is the god of

writing.

Linguistics = Practice

your DJEHUTY once a

day. I DJEHUTY

sanskrita very well.